WAITING
ON GOD
ANDREW
MURRAY

Books by Andrew Murray

The Blood of Christ
Mighty Is Your Hand (edited by Hazard)
Raising Your Child to Love God
Revival
Waiting on God

Andrew Murray Christian Maturity Library

The Believer's Absolute Surrender
The Believer's Secret of Holiness
The Believer's Secret of Spiritual Power (with Finney)
The Spirit of Christ

Andrew Murray Prayer Library

The Believer's Prayer Life
The Believer's School of Prayer
The Ministry of Intercessory Prayer

WAITING ON GOD
ANDREW MURRAY

A CLASSIC DEVOTIONAL
EDITED FOR TODAY'S READER

BETHANYHOUSE
Minneapolis, Minnesota

Waiting on God
by Andrew Murray

Copyright © 1986, 2001
Bethany House Publishers

Edited and updated for today's reader, 2001.
Previously published by Bethany House Publishers under the title
The Believer's Secret of Waiting on God.

Cover design by Eric Walljasper

Scripture quotation credits are located at the back of the book.

Published by Bethany House Publishers
A Ministry of Bethany Fellowship International
11400 Hampshire Avenue South
Bloomington, Minnesota 55438
www.bethanyhouse.com

Printed in the United States of America by
Bethany Press International, Bloomington, Minnesota 55438

Library of Congress Cataloging-in-Publication Data

Murray, Andrew, 1828–1917.
    Waiting on God / by Andrew Murray.—Newly edited and updated.
        p. cm.
Rev. ed. of: The believer's secret of waiting on God. 1986.
    ISBN 0-7642-2469-7 (pbk.)
    1. Trust in God—Christianity. I. Murray, Andrew, 1828–1917.
Believer's secret of waiting on God. II. Title.
    BV4637 .M795 2001
    248.4—dc21
                                                            2001001319

ANDREW MURRAY was born in South Africa in 1828. After receiving his education in Scotland and Holland, he returned to South Africa and spent many years as both pastor and missionary. He was a staunch advocate of biblical Christianity. He is best known for his many devotional books.

"Wait Only Upon God"

*My soul, wait silently for God alone, for my
expectation is from Him.*

Psalm 62:5

*Since ancient times no one has heard, no ear has perceived, no
eye has seen any God besides you, who acts on behalf
of those who wait for him.*

Isaiah 64:4 NIV

Wait only upon God; my soul, be still,
And let thy God unfold His perfect will.
Thou fain wouldst follow Him throughout this year,
Thou fain with listening heart His voice would hear,
Thou fain wouldst be a passive instrument
Possessed by God and ever Spirit-sent
Upon His service sweet—then be thou still,
For only thus can He in thee fulfill
His heart's desire. Oh, hinder not His hand
From fashioning the vessel He hath planned.
"Be silent unto God," and thou shalt know

The quiet, holy calm He doth bestow
On those who wait on Him; so shalt thou bear
His presence, and His life and light e'en where
The night is darkest, and thine earthly days
Shall show His love and sound His glorious praise.
And He will work with hand unfettered, free,
His high and holy purposes through thee.
First *on* thee must that hand of power be turned,
Till in His love's strong fire thy dross is burned,
And thou come forth a vessel for thy Lord,
So frail and empty, yet, since He hath poured
Into thine emptiness His life, His love,
Henceforth through thee the power of God shall move
And He will work *for* thee. Stand still and see
The victories thy God will gain for thee;
So silent, yet so irresistible,
Thy God shall do the thing impossible.
Oh, question not henceforth what thou canst do;
Thou canst do *nought*. But He will carry through
The work where human energy had failed
Where all thy best endeavors had availed
Thee nothing. Then, my soul, wait and be still;
Thy God shall work for thee His perfect will.
If thou wilt take no less, *His best* shall be
Thy portion now and through eternity.

—Freda Hanbury

Extract from an address
in Exeter Hall
May 31, 1895

Nothing has surprised me more than the letters that have come to me from missionaries and others around the world, devoted men and women, testifying to the need they feel in their work for a deeper and a clearer insight into all that Christ can be to them. Let us look to God to reveal himself among His people in a measure very few have realized. Let us expect great things of our God. At all our conventions and assemblies too little time is given to *waiting on God*. Is He not willing to put things right in His own divine way? Has the life of God's people reached the limit of what God is willing to do for them? Surely not. We want to wait on Him; to put away

our experiences, however blessed they have been; our concep-
tions of truth, however sound and scriptural we think they
seem; our plans, however needful and suitable they appear;
and give God time and place to show us what He can do, what
He will do. God has new developments and new resources. He
can do new things, unheard-of things, hidden things. Let us
enlarge our hearts and not limit Him.

"For when you did awesome things that we did not expect,
you came down, and the mountains trembled before you"
(Isaiah 64:3).

—Andrew Murray

Contents

Preface

I was recently impressed by the thought that in all our Christian life, personal and public, we need more of God. I feel that we need to train our people in their worship to wait on God and also to cultivate a deeper sense of His presence, of more direct contact with Him, and of entire dependence on Him as a definite aim of our ministry. In my message given in Exeter Hall, I expressed this simple thought in connection with our Christian work. I was surprised at the response. I saw that God's Spirit had been working the same desire in many hearts.

The experiences of the past year, both personal and public, have greatly deepened this conviction. It is as if I am only beginning to see the deep truth concerning our relationship to God being centered on waiting on Him, and how little we have been sensitive to this need in our life and work. The following pages are the outcome of my conviction and of my desire to direct the attention of all believers to the one great remedy for all our needs. More than half of these chapters were written while aboard ship. I send them out with the prayer that He who loves to use the weak may give His blessing with them.

I do not know if it will be possible for me to put into a few words the chief things we need to learn. In a note on William Law at the close of this book, I have mentioned some. But what I want to say here is this: The great lack of our Christianity today is that we do not *know God.* The answer to every complaint of weakness and failure, the message to every congregation or convention seeking instruction on holiness, should simply be "Where is your God?" If you really believe in God and His power, He will put it right. God is willing and able by His Holy Spirit. Stop expecting the solution to come from yourself, or the answer from anything there is in man, and simply yield yourself completely to God to work in and through you. He will do it all.

How simple this sounds! And yet it is the gospel we know so little about. I can only cast these less-than-perfect meditations on the love of my brethren and of our God. May He use them to draw us to himself, to learn in practice and experience the blessed art of *waiting on God.* Pray that we might grasp the influence a life spent wholly waiting upon God could have, not by thought or imagination or effort, but by the power of the Holy Spirit.

With greetings in Christ to all God's saints it has been my privilege to meet, and no less to those I have not met, I offer myself, your brother and servant,

Andrew Murray

The God of Our Salvation

Truly my soul silently waits for God; from Him comes my salvation.

Psalm 62:1

If salvation indeed comes from God, and is entirely His work, just as our creation was, it follows that our first and highest duty is to wait on Him to do the work that pleases Him. Waiting then becomes the only way to experience full salvation, the only way to truly know God as the God of our salvation. All the difficulties that are brought forward, keeping us back from full salvation, have their cause in this one thing: our lack of knowledge and practice of waiting on God. All that the church and its members need for the manifestation of the mighty power of God in the world is the return to our true place, the place that belongs to us, both in creation and redemption, the place of absolute and unceasing dependence on God. Let us

Waiting on God: To experience full salvation. The only way to truly know God. We miss blessings because we fail to wait on God

strive to see what the elements are that make up this most blessed and needful waiting on God. It may help us to look into the reasons why this grace is so neglected and to feel how infinitely desirable it is that the church, that is we believers, should learn this blessed secret at any price.

The deep need for this waiting on God lies equally in the nature of man and in the nature of God. God, as Creator, formed man to be a vessel in which He could show forth His power and goodness. Man was not to have in himself a fountain of life, or strength, or happiness. The ever-living and only living One was intended each moment to be the communicator to man of all that he needed. Man's glory and blessedness was not to be independent, or dependent upon himself, but dependent on a God of such infinite riches and love. Man was to have the joy of receiving every moment out of the fullness of God. This was his blessed state before the Fall.

When he turned from God, he was still absolutely dependent on Him. There was not the slightest hope of his recovery from the state of death, except in God, His power and His mercy. It is God alone who began the work of redemption. It is God alone who continues and carries it on each moment in each individual believer. Even in the regenerate man there is no power of goodness in himself. He has and can have nothing except what he each moment receives while waiting on God. This is indispensable and must be as continuous and unbroken as the breathing that maintains his natural life.

Because believers do not know their relationship to God of absolute poverty and helplessness, they have no sense of the

The Lord our God is the communicator of all that we need

need of absolute and unceasing dependence, or the unspeakable blessedness of continual waiting on God. But once a believer begins to see it, and consent to it, he by the Holy Spirit begins each moment to receive what God each moment works. Waiting on God becomes his brightest hope and joy. As he understands how God, as God, as infinite love, delights to impart His own nature to His child as fully as He can, how God is not weary of each moment keeping charge of his life and strength, he wonders how he ever thought otherwise of God than as a God to be waited on all day long. God unceasingly gives and works as His child unceasingly waits and receives. This is the blessed life.

"Truly my soul silently waits for God; from Him comes my salvation." First we wait on God for salvation. Then we learn that salvation is only to bring us to God and teach us to wait on Him. Then we find what is better still: that waiting on God is itself the highest salvation. It is ascribing to Him the glory of being all; it is experiencing that He is all to us. May God teach us the blessedness of waiting on Him!

My soul, wait only on God!

In waiting on God and we receive from him there is true blessedness.

True blessedness comes from waiting on God.

The Keynote of Life

I have waited for your salvation, O LORD.

Genesis 49:18

It is not easy to say in exactly what sense Jacob used these words that appear right in the middle of his prophecies regarding the future of his sons. But they do certainly indicate that both for himself and for them his expectation was from God alone. It was God's salvation Jacob waited for, a salvation God had promised and that God alone could work out. Jacob knew he and his sons were under God's charge. Jehovah, the everlasting God, would show them what His saving power was and what it could do. The words point forward to that wonderful story of redemption that is not yet finished and to the glorious future in eternity where our redemption leads. They suggest to us that there is no salvation but God's salvation, and waiting on God for it, whether for our personal experience or for the world around us, is our first duty.

Let us think of the inconceivably glorious salvation God

Meditate in the Word of God
We are to surrender ourselves to God.

has accomplished for us in Christ and is now purposing to work out and perfect in us by His Spirit. Let us meditate until we begin to realize that participation in this great salvation must be the work of God himself. God cannot separate himself from His grace, or goodness, or strength as an external thing, such as the rain He gives from heaven. He can only give it as an extension of himself, and we can only enjoy it as He works it directly and continually in us. And the only reason He does not work it more effectually and continuously is that we do not allow Him to. We hinder Him either by our indifference or by our self-effort, so that He cannot do what He desires. What He asks of us, in the way of surrender, obedience, and trust, is all comprised in this one phrase: waiting on Him for His salvation. It combines the deep sense of our entire helplessness to work what is divinely good and our perfect confidence that God will work it all by His divine power.

Again, I say, let us meditate on the divine glory of the salvation God purposes to work out in us, until we know the truths it implies. Our heart is the scene of a divine operation more wonderful than creation. We can do as little toward the work as we could toward creating the world, except as God works in us to will and to do. God only asks us to yield, to consent, to wait on Him, and He will do it all. Let us meditate and be still until we see how proper and right and blessed it is that God alone does it all. Then our soul will drop down in deep humility and say, "I have waited for your salvation, O LORD." And the deep, blessed foundation of all our praying

Obedience the Lord
Trust the Lord

and working will be: "Truly my soul silently waits for God" (Psalm 62:1).

The application of the truth to wider circles, to those we labor among or intercede for, to the church of Christ around us, or throughout the world, is not difficult. There can be no good except what God works; to wait on God and to have the heart filled with faith in His working, and in that faith to pray for His mighty power to come down, is our only wisdom. Oh, for the eyes of our heart to be opened to see God working in us and in others, and to see how blessed it is to worship and simply wait for His salvation!

Our private and public prayers are our chief expression of our relationship to God. It is mainly in them that our waiting on God must be exercised. If our waiting begins by quieting the activities of daily life and being still before God; if we bow and seek to see God in His universal and almighty operation; if we yield to Him in the assurance that He is working and will work in us; if we maintain the place of humility and stillness, and surrender until God's Spirit has stirred up in us confidence that He will perfect His work, our waiting will become the strength and the joy of our soul. Life will become one deep cry: "I have waited for your salvation, O LORD."

My soul, wait only on God!

The True Place of the Creature

*These all wait for You, that You may give them their food in
due season. What You give them they gather in; You open
Your hand, they are filled with good.*

Psalm 104:27–28

This psalm, in praise of the Creator, has been speaking of the
birds and the beasts of the forest; of the young lions, and of
man going forth to his work; of the great sea, in which there
are innumerable creeping organisms, both small and large.
And it sums up the whole relationship of all creation to its
Creator, and its continuous and universal dependence on
Him, in the one phrase: "These all wait for You!" Just as much
as it was God's work to create, it is His work to maintain. As
little as the creature could create itself, is it left to provide for
itself. The whole creation is ruled by the one unalterable law
of *waiting on God*!

The phrase is the simple expression of the very reason for which the creature was brought into existence, the very foundation of its makeup. The one purpose for which God gave life to creatures was that in them He might prove and show forth His wisdom, power, and goodness, in His being each moment their life and happiness, and in pouring out to them, according to their capacity, the riches of His goodness and power. And just as this is the place and nature of God, to be the constant supplier of everything the creature needs, so the place and nature of the creature is nothing but this: to wait on God and receive from Him what He alone can and delights to give.

If through this book we hope to grasp what *waiting on God* is to the believer, to practice it and to experience its blessing, it is necessary for us to begin at the very beginning and see the deep reasonableness of the call that comes to us. We will come to understand how the duty is not an arbitrary command. And we will see how it is not only made necessary by our sin and helplessness but it is also our restoration to our original destiny and our highest rank, to our true place and glory as creatures happily dependent on the all-glorious God.

If our eyes are once opened to this precious truth, all nature will become a preacher, reminding us of the relationship that was begun in creation and is continued in grace. As we read this psalm and learn to look on all of life in nature as continually maintained by God, waiting on Him will be seen as the greatest need of our being. As we think of the young lions and the ravens crying to Him, of the birds and the fish and every insect waiting on Him until He gives them their food in due season, we will see that the very nature and glory of God is that He is a God who is to be waited on. Every thought of what nature is and what God is will give new impetus to the call: "Wait only upon God" (Psalm 62:5 KJV).

"These all wait for You, That You may give them their food in due season" (Psalm 104:27). It is God who gives all: let this truth enter deeply into our hearts. Until we fully understand all that is implied in our waiting on God, and until we have been able to cultivate the habit, let the truth enter our souls. Waiting continually on the one true God in entire dependence upon Him is the only true religion. It is the one unalterable and all-comprehensive expression of our true relationship to the One in whom we live.

Let us resolve once and for all that it will be the one characteristic of our life and worship to continually, humbly, and honestly wait on God. We may rest assured that the One who made us for himself that He might give himself to us and dwell in us will *never* disappoint us. In waiting on Him we will find rest and joy and strength and the supply of every need.

My soul, wait only on God!

Waiting on God for Supplies

The LORD upholds all who fall, and raises up all who are bowed down. The eyes of all look expectantly to You, and You give them their food in due season.

Psalm 145:14–15

Psalm 104 is a psalm of creation, and the words "these all wait for You" are used in reference to the animal creation. Psalm 145 is a psalm of the kingdom, and "the eyes of all look expectantly to You" refers specifically to the needs of God's people, particularly those who have fallen or are discouraged. What the universe and the animal creation do unconsciously, God's people are to do intelligently and voluntarily. Man is to be the interpreter of nature. He is to prove that there is nothing nobler or more blessed in the exercise of our free will than to wait on God.

If an army has been sent out to march into enemy territory and news is received that it is not advancing, the question is at once asked, "What is the cause of the delay?" The answer will very often be: "Waiting for supplies." If provisions of gear or ammunition have not arrived, they dare not proceed. It is no different in the Christian life: Day by day we need our supplies from above. And there is nothing so necessary as cultivating a spirit of dependence on God and of confidence in Him that refuses to go on without the needed supply of grace and strength.

If you ask whether this is different from waiting on God in the place prayer, I answer that there can be a lot of praying going on without really waiting on God. In prayer, we are often occupied with ourselves, with our own needs and our own efforts to effectively present them. In waiting on God, the first thought is of God himself. We enter His presence and immediately feel the need to be quiet, so that He can speak to us. God longs to reveal himself to us and to fill us with himself. Waiting on God gives Him time, in His own way and divine power, to come to us.

It is especially at the time of prayer that we ought to cultivate this spirit of quiet waiting.

Before you pray, bow quietly before God; remember and realize who He is, how near He is, how certainly He can and will help. Be still before Him and allow His Holy Spirit to awaken in your soul the childlike disposition of absolute dependence and confident expectation. Wait on God as you would a living person. He is the living God who is aware of you and is longing to fill all of your needs. Wait on God until you know you have met Him; your prayer time will never be the same.

And when you pray, allow intervals of silence, reverent stillness of soul in which you yield yourself to God. He may have something He wishes to teach you or to work in you. Waiting on Him will become the most blessed part of prayer, and the answer to your prayer will be twice as precious because it is the fruit of fellowship with Him. God has ordained that in harmony with His holy nature and our humble estate we honor Him by waiting on Him. Let us give Him this service gladly and honestly. He will reward it abundantly.

"These all wait for You, that You may give them their food in due season" (Psalm 104:27). God provides in nature for the creatures He has made. How much more will He provide in grace for those He has redeemed! Learn to say about every want, failure, or lack of the grace you need: I have waited too little on God. He would have given me in due season all I needed.

My soul, wait only on God!

—Day 5—

Waiting on God for Instruction

Show me Your ways, O LORD; teach me Your paths. Lead me in Your truth and teach me, for You are the God of my salvation; on You I wait all the day.

Psalm 25:4–5

We spoke yesterday about an army at the point of entering enemy territory whose reason for delay was "waiting for supplies." Their answer could as well have been "waiting for instruction" or "waiting for orders." If the last dispatch had not been received with the final orders of the commander in chief, the army would not have dared to move forward. It is the same in the Christian life. Waiting for instruction is as important as waiting for supplies.

This fact is shown beautifully in Psalm 25. The writer knew and loved God's law supremely and meditated on it day and night. He also knew this was not enough. To rightly grasp the truth and personally apply it to his own circumstances, he needed divine instruction.

This psalm is distinctive because of the author's repeated expression of his need for divine teaching and his childlike confidence that it would be given. Study the psalm until your heart is filled with two thoughts: the absolute need for divine guidance and the absolute certainty of receiving it. It is with these thoughts in mind that the psalmist declares, "On You I wait all the day." Waiting for guidance or instruction throughout the day is a very blessed part of waiting on God.

The Father in heaven is so interested in His children and so longs to have them in step with His will and His love that He is willing to hold their guidance in His own hands. He knows so well that we do not naturally do what is holy except when He works it in us, that He makes His demands the same as promises of what He will do to watch over us and lead us through the day. We may count on Him to teach us His way and to show us His path not only in special trials and hard times but also in everyday life.

Are we convinced that the way to receive this guidance is by daily waiting on Him for instruction? We must acknowledge our need and declare our faith in His help. We will have a deep, restful assurance that He hears and answers. "The humble He teaches His way" (Psalm 25:9).

"On You I wait all the day." As simple as it is to walk all day in the light of the sun, it can become simple and delightful for a soul who has practiced waiting on God to walk all day in the enjoyment of God's light and leading. The one thing needed for such a life is the knowledge and faith that God is our only source of wisdom and goodness. If we could truly see God's love for us, and if we truly believed that He waits to be our life and to work His will in us, waiting on God would become our highest joy, the natural, spontaneous response of our heart.

My soul, wait only on God!

— *Day 6* —

Waiting on God for All the Saints

*O my God, I trust in You; let me not be ashamed; let not my
enemies triumph over me. Indeed, let no one who waits on
You be ashamed; let those be ashamed who deal
treacherously without cause.*

Psalm 25:2–3

In our meditation for today, let each one of us forget himself
and think of the great number of God's people throughout the
world who are waiting on Him right now. And let us all join
in this fervent prayer for each other: "Let no one who waits
on You be ashamed."

Think for a moment of the multitudes of people who need
that prayer; how many there are who are sick and weary and
alone, and who feel that their prayers are not being answered,
who sometimes fear that their hope is in vain. Remember, too,
the many servants of God, ministers or missionaries, teachers

or workers, whose hope in their work has been disappointed and whose longing for a manifestation of God's power and blessing remains unsatisfied. Think of those who have heard of this life of rest and perfect peace, of abiding light and fellowship, of strength and victory, but who cannot find the path to it. In each of these cases there is no explanation but that they have not yet learned the secret of waiting on God. They simply need what we all need: the full assurance that waiting on God is never an exercise in vain. Let us remember those who are tempted to give up or who are growing weary of the struggle, and unite in the cry, "Let no one who waits on You be ashamed [or disappointed]."

If this intercession for others becomes a part of our waiting on Him, we will help to bear each other's burdens and so fulfill the law of Christ.

There will be introduced into our waiting on God that element of unselfishness and love that is the path to the highest blessing and the fullest communion with God. Love for our neighbor and love for God are inseparably linked. In God, the love for His Son and for us is *one* "that the love with which You loved Me may be in them, and I in them" (John 17:26). In Christ, the love of the Father for Him and His love for *us* is *one*: "As the Father loved Me, I also have loved you; abide in My love" (John 15:9). He asks us to allow His love for us to carry over to our neighbor: "A new commandment I give to you, that you love one another; as I have loved you, that you also love one another" (John 13:34). The love of God and of Christ is inseparably linked with love for our neighbor.

How can we prove and cultivate this love in any other way than by daily praying for each other? Christ did not seek to enjoy the Father's love for himself alone; He passed it on to us. So let us also love our neighbor.

"Let no one who waits on You be ashamed." Twice in this psalm David speaks of waiting on God for himself; here he thinks of all those who wait on Him. Let this be a reminder to all God's children who are weary or who are going through trials that there are more people praying for them than they know. Let it move them and us, so that in our waiting we can at times forget our own needs and say to the Father, "These also wait on you. Answer them." Let it inspire us all with new courage—for who is there who is not at times tired and discouraged? "Let no one who waits on You be ashamed" is a promise in a prayer, for those who wait on God will not be disappointed. Many have found for themselves that God strengthens those who wait: "Wait on the LORD; be of good courage, and He shall strengthen your heart" (Psalm 27:14).

Blessed Father, we humbly ask you, fulfill your Word and let none who wait on you be ashamed or disappointed. Some are weary, and waiting seems long and painful. Some are weak and scarcely know how to wait. And some are so entangled in the *effort* of their prayers that they think they do not have the time to wait. Father, teach us all how to wait. Teach us to think of each other and pray for each other more often. Teach us to think of *you*, the God of all who wait, and none of us will be disappointed. For Jesus' sake. Amen.

My soul, wait only on God!

Our Plea in Prayer While We Wait

Let integrity and uprightness preserve me, for I wait for You.

Psalm 25:21

This is the third mention of the word *wait* in this psalm. As in verse 5, "On You do I wait all the day," so here, too, the believer appeals to God to remember that he is waiting on Him for an answer. It is a good thing for a soul not only to wait on God but also to be filled with such childlike confidence as to say, "Lord, you know I am waiting on you!"

The prayer of our text is one of great importance in our spiritual life. If we draw near to God, it must be with a true heart. There must be perfect integrity and uprightness in our dealings with God. In the next psalm, we read, "But as for me, I will walk in my integrity; redeem me and be merciful to me" (Psalm 26:11). God seeks the single-hearted—"Continue Your lovingkindness to those who know You, and Your righteousness to the upright in heart" (Psalm 36:10)—the soul who allows nothing sinful or even doubtful to enter. If it is to meet with the Holy One and receive His full blessing, it must be with a heart wholly given up to His will. The attitude that enables us in our waiting must be one of integrity and uprightness.

And if in our first attempt to truly live a life of waiting on God we discover how much we are lacking in perfect integrity, this will be one of the blessings of our attempt. A soul cannot seek close fellowship with God or attain to a consciousness of waiting on Him without an honest and entire surrender to His will.

It is not only in connection with the prayer of our text but also with every prayer that surrender to His will is appropriate. And then it must be clear *what* we are waiting for, not simply that we are waiting. It may be that we long for a sense of His holy presence and nearness. Or we may have a special petition for which we need a precise answer. Perhaps our whole inner life thirsts for a manifestation of God's power. Beyond our own needs, we may pray for the state of the church, and God's people, or some part of His work. It is good that we sometimes take stock of exactly what we are waiting for and then renew our intention to wait only on *Him* for the answer.

This brings us to think about *who* we are waiting on—not an idol, a god we have conjured up by our poor concept of who He is. Let us acknowledge Him as the living God in His great glory, infinite holiness, power, wisdom, goodness, and love. Let us be still and wait and worship until we know He is near and then say, "It is on *you* that I wait."

Waiting requires time and patience. There is no quick way to wait on God. It implies sacrifice and separation, a soul entirely given up to God to wait expectantly and with genuine faith and not to dictate what He will do or say. It is our privilege and joy to be in His presence. We will be changed even if we have not uttered one word of supplication.

My soul, wait only on God!

Be Strong and of Good Courage

Wait on the LORD; be of good courage, and He shall strengthen your heart; wait, I say, on the LORD!

Psalm 27:14

The psalmist said in the previous verse, "I would have lost heart, unless I had believed that I would see the goodness of the LORD in the land of the living." If it had not been for his faith in God, his heart would have given up. But in the confident assurance in God that faith gives, he urges himself and us to remember one thing above all—to wait on God. We will not be disappointed. One of the greatest needs in our waiting on God, and one of the deepest secrets of its blessedness, is a quiet, confident persuasion that our waiting is not in vain: courage to believe that God will hear and help.

"Be of good courage." These words are frequently found in connection with some great combat with strong enemies and the utter insufficiency of all human strength. Is waiting on God so difficult that such words are needed? The deliverance we often wait for is from our enemies, in whose presence we are powerless. The blessings we plead for are spiritual and unseen; things impossible with men; heavenly, supernatural, divine. Our heart may well faint and fail. Our souls are unaccustomed to holding intimate fellowship with God. The God we wait on often appears to hide. And so we are often tempted to fear that we are not waiting correctly, that our faith is too weak, that our desire is not as pure or as earnest as it should be, or that our surrender is not complete. In the middle of all these fears or doubts, what a blessing it is to hear the voice of God: "Wait on the LORD; be of good courage, and He shall strengthen your heart." Let nothing keep you from waiting on God in full assurance that it is worthwhile.

The one lesson our text teaches us is that when we set ourselves to wait on God, we should resolve beforehand that it will be with the most confident expectation of God's meeting us and blessing us. We should make up our minds that nothing is ever so sure as the fact that waiting on God will bring us untold blessing. We are in such a habit of evaluating God and His work in us by what we *feel* that it is very likely that on some occasions we will be discouraged because we do not feel any special blessing. Above everything, when you wait on God, do so in the spirit of hope. It is God in His glory, His power, and His love who is longing to bless you.

If you say you are afraid of deceiving yourself with false hope because you do not see or feel any valid reason for such expectations, my answer is: *God* is the valid reason for your expecting great things. You are not waiting on yourself to see what you feel and what changes come about. You are waiting on God, first to know what He is, and then what He will do. The blessedness of waiting on God has its root in the fact that He is such a blessed being, full of goodness and power and life and joy. And we, however wretched, cannot come into contact with Him without that life and power entering into us and blessing us. God is love! That is the one and only all-sufficient reason for your expectation. Love seeks out its own: God's delight is to impart himself to His children. Come. However weak you *feel*, wait in His presence. Just as a weak and sickly invalid is brought out into the sunshine to allow its healing warmth to go through his body, come with all that is dark and cold in you into the sunshine of God's holy, omnipotent love, and sit and wait there. As the sun does its work in the weak who seek its rays, God will do His work in you. Trust Him! "Wait on the Lord; be of good courage, and He shall strengthen your heart."

My soul, wait only on God!

Waiting on God With the Whole Heart

Be of good courage, and He shall strengthen your heart,
all you who hope in the LORD.

Psalm 31:24

Our text is nearly the same as the one in our last chapter. But I will take advantage of the words again to press home a much-needed lesson for all who desire to truly know what it is to wait on God. The lesson is this: It is with the *whole heart* that we must wait. "Be of good courage, and He shall strengthen your *heart*." The fruit of our waiting depends on the state of our heart. As a man's heart is, so is he before God. We can advance no further or deeper into the Holy Place of God's presence than our heart is prepared for it by the Holy Spirit.

This truth appears so simple that some may ask, "Isn't it obvious? Why insist on it so specifically?" It is because many

Christians have no sense of the difference between waiting with the mind and waiting with the heart, and the former is far more diligently cultivated than the latter. They have not grasped how infinitely greater the heart is than the mind. It is the primary cause of weakness in our Christian life, and it is only as this is understood that waiting on God will have its full blessing.

Proverbs 3:5 may help to clarify the point: "Trust in the LORD with all your heart, and lean not on your own understanding" (Proverbs 3:5). In any faith experience we must use both powers. The mind gathers knowledge from God's Word and prepares the "food" with which the heart is to be nourished. But there is the danger of leaning on our own understanding and trusting in our own comprehension of divine things. People generally think that if they give mental attention to the truth, the spiritual life will take care of itself. This is by no means the case. The understanding deals with concepts of divine things, but it cannot reach the life of the soul. Hence the command: "Trust in the LORD with all your *heart*." It is with the heart that man believes and comes into contact with God. It is in the heart that God has given His Holy Spirit to reveal the presence and power of God working in us. In our efforts to follow God, it is the heart that must trust, love, worship, and obey. The mind is completely incapable of creating or maintaining the spiritual life. It is the heart that must wait on God.

It is the same in the physical life. My mind may dictate what to eat and drink and even understand how the food nourishes me. But reason cannot do the nourishing. The body's organs are for that purpose. And so reason may tell me what God's Word says, but it can do nothing about feeding my soul with the bread of life—the heart alone can do this by faith and trust in God. A man may study the nature and effects of food or sleep, but when he wants to eat or sleep he sets aside his thoughts and study and allows the power of his body to do the eating or sleeping. And so the Christian, when he has studied or heard God's Word, must set aside his thoughts and awaken his heart to God and seek a living fellowship with Him.

Here is the blessing of waiting on God: to be able to confess the inability of my thoughts and efforts to accomplish what only the heart can appropriate, and to free myself to bow before Him in holy silence, trusting Him to renew and strengthen His work in me. Remember the difference between *knowing* with the mind and *believing* with the heart. Beware of the temptation to lean on your understanding. Present your heart to Him as that wonderful part of your spiritual nature in which God reveals himself and by which you can know Him. Develop confidence that though you cannot see into your heart, God is working there by His Holy Spirit. Allow the heart to wait at times in perfect silence and quiet; in its hidden depths God will work. Be confident of this. Give your whole heart, with its secret workings, into God's hands continually. He wants possession of your heart and He will take it.

My soul, wait only on God!

Waiting on God in Humble Fear and Hope

Behold, the eye of the LORD is on those who fear Him, on those who hope in His mercy, to deliver their soul from death, and to keep them alive in famine. Our soul waits for the LORD; He is our help and our shield. For our heart shall rejoice in Him, because we have trusted in His holy name. Let Your mercy, O LORD, be upon us, just as we hope in You.

Psalm 33:18–22

God's eye is on His people; their eye is on Him. When we wait on God, we are looking up to Him, but He is also looking down on us. The blessedness of waiting on God is that it takes our eyes and thoughts away from ourselves, even our needs and desires, and occupies them with God alone. Let us consider this wonderful meeting between God and His people and carefully notice what we are taught here about those on whom God's eye rests.

"Behold, the eye of the LORD is on those who fear Him,

on those who hope in His mercy." Fear and hope are generally thought to be in conflict with each other. In the presence and worship of God, they are found side by side in perfect harmony. In God, all apparent contradictions are reconciled: righteousness and peace, judgment and mercy, holiness and love, infinite power and infinite gentleness. There is a fear of punishment that is cast out entirely by perfect love. But there is another fear that speaks of awe and respect. In the song of Moses and the Lamb they sang, "Who shall not fear You, O Lord, and glorify Your name?" (Revelation 15:4). "Then a voice came from the throne, saying, 'Praise our God, all you His servants and those who fear Him, both small and great!' " (Revelation 19:5). Let us in our waiting always seek to "fear this glorious and awesome name, the LORD your God" (Deuteronomy 28:58). The deeper we bow before His holiness in reverent fear and adoring awe, even as the angels veil their faces before the throne, the more will His holiness be revealed to us. The deeper we enter into the truth "that no flesh should glory in His presence" (1 Corinthians 1:29), to that degree will we be permitted to see His glory. "Behold, the eye of the LORD is on those who fear Him, on those who hope in His mercy" (Psalm 33:18).

The true fear of God does not keep us from hope. On the contrary, it stimulates and strengthens hope. The lower we bow before Him, the deeper we feel we have nothing to hope in but His mercy and the bolder we are to trust Him. Let every exercise of waiting on God be pervaded by abounding hope— a hope as bright and boundless as God's mercy. The fatherly kindness of God is such that in whatever state we come to Him we may confidently hope in His mercy.

Think about the God on whom we wait: His eye is on those who fear Him, on those who hope in His mercy to deliver them and to keep them alive. He doesn't say He will always prevent the *danger* of death and famine—this is sometimes needed to stir up men to wait on Him—but He does say He will deliver them and keep them alive. The dangers are often very real and dark; the situation, whether in the natural or spiritual life, may appear to be utterly hopeless. But there is always hope: God's eye is on us.

His eye sees the danger, and in tender love He sees His trembling child. He sees the moment when the heart is ripe for the blessing and the best way that it should come. Let us fear God and hope in His mercy! And let us humbly but boldly say, "We wait for the Lord. He is our help and our shield."

We are blessed to wait on such a God, who is present to help in time of trouble, our protector and defender against every danger. Children of God, we must learn to reach the point of entire helplessness and in stillness wait to see the salvation of God. In the driest spiritual famine, and even when death appears to have the upper hand, wait on God! He does deliver. He does keep us alive. Say this not only when you are alone but also say it to each other—the psalm speaks not of *one*, but of God's people: "*Our* soul waits . . ." Strengthen and encourage each other in the holy exercise of waiting, that each person may say not only of himself but also of his fellow believers, "*We* have waited for Him; *we* will be glad and rejoice in His salvation."

My soul, wait only on God!

Waiting Patiently
on God

*Rest in the LORD, and wait patiently for Him; do not
fret because of him who prospers in his way, because
of the man who brings wicked schemes to pass. For evildoers
shall be cut off; but those who wait on the LORD,
they shall inherit the earth.*

Psalm 37:7, 9

"By your patience possess your souls" (Luke 21:19). "For you
have need of endurance" (Hebrews 10:36). "But let patience
have *its* perfect work, that you may be perfect and complete,
lacking nothing" (James 1:4). Through these words, the Holy
Spirit shows us how important patience and endurance are in
the Christian life. And nowhere is there a better place for cultivating or displaying it than in waiting on God. There we discover how impatient we are and how our impatience affects
our life. We confess at times that we are impatient with others

and with circumstances that hinder us or with our slow progress in the Christian life. And if we truly set ourselves to wait on God, we will find that we are impatient with Him because He does not immediately, or as soon as we would like, give us what we ask. It is in waiting on God that our eyes are opened to believe in His wise and sovereign will and to see that the sooner and more completely we yield to it, the more surely His blessing will come to us.

"So then it is not of him who wills, nor of him who runs, but of God who shows mercy" (Romans 9:16). We have as little power to increase or strengthen our spiritual life as we had to originate it. We "were born, not of blood, nor of the will of the flesh, nor of the will of man, but of God" (John 1:13). So, all our willing and running, our desire and effort accomplish nothing; it is God who accomplishes and who shows mercy. All the exercises of the spiritual life—our reading and praying, our going and doing—have their own value. But they can go no further than this: they point the way and prepare us in humility to look to and depend on God alone and in patience to wait for His time and mercy. The waiting is to teach us our absolute dependence upon God's working and to patiently place ourselves at His disposal. They that wait on the Lord shall inherit the land: the Promised Land and its blessing. The heirs must wait; they can afford to wait.

"Rest in the Lord, and wait patiently for Him." Scholars say that "rest in the Lord" may also be interpreted "keep silent before the Lord" or "be still before the Lord." It is resting in the Lord, in His will, His promises, His faithfulness, and His love, that makes patience easy. And resting in Him is nothing but being silent before Him and having our thoughts and wishes, our fears and hopes hushed into calm and quiet by that great peace of God that passes all understanding. That peace keeps the heart and mind when we are anxious about anything, because we have made our requests known to Him. The rest, the silence, the stillness, the patient waiting—all find their strength and joy in God himself.

The need for patience as well as the reasonableness and blessedness of patience will be made clear to the waiting soul. Our patience will be seen to be the counterpart of God's patience. He longs to bless us far more than we desire it. But as the farmer has great patience waiting for the fruit to ripen, so God accommodates our slowness to learn and bears with our weaknesses. Let us remember this and be encouraged to wait patiently. The Lord will bring results *in its time* (Isaiah 60:22).

Rest, then, and wait. Seek not only the help or the gift, but seek *Him*. Give God glory by resting in Him, trusting Him, and waiting for Him. Patience honors Him; it allows Him to do His work, yielding self wholly into His hands. It lets God *be God*. If your waiting is for some particular request, wait patiently. If your waiting is the exercise of the spiritual life seeking to know and have more of God, wait patiently. Whether it is in the designated periods of waiting or the continuous habit of the soul, rest in the Lord, be still before Him, and wait patiently. You will inherit the land—and all else that God has planned for you.

My soul, wait only on God!

Keeping All His Ways

*Wait on the LORD, and keep His way, and He shall
exalt you to inherit the land.*

Psalm 37:34

If we want to find someone, we ask where he lives and how to get there. When we wait on God, we must be sure we are in His way; outside of it we cannot expect to find Him. "You meet him who rejoices and does righteousness, who remembers You in Your ways" (Isaiah 64:5).

The connection is very close between the two parts of the command in our text: "Wait on the LORD"—having to do with worship and attitude—"and keep His way"—dealing with our walk and work. The outer life must be in harmony with the inner life; the inner is the inspiration and the strength for the outer. God has made known in His Word His way for our conduct and invites our confidence that His grace and help will come when we need it. If we do not keep His way, our waiting on Him will be futile. Surrender in full obedience to all His will is the secret of access to the blessings of His fellowship.

Notice how strongly this comes out in Psalm 37: "Wait on the LORD, and keep His way, and He shall exalt you to inherit the land; when the wicked are cut off, you shall see it. I have seen the wicked in great power, and spreading himself like a native green tree. Yet he passed away, and behold, he was no more; indeed I sought him, but he could not be found." When we see men around us prosperous and happy while they forsake God's ways, and ourselves in difficulty or suffering, we are tempted to be troubled at what appears unjust, and may even yield to finding prosperity in *their* path. The psalmist says, "Do not fret because of evildoers, nor be envious of the workers of iniquity. For they shall soon be cut down like the grass, and wither as the green herb. Trust in the LORD, and do good; dwell in the land, and feed on His faithfulness" (37:1–3). Do what God asks *you* to do; He will do more for you than you can ask.

Do not harbor the fear that you cannot keep His way. None of us has the strength in ourselves, but if we surrender to God and trust Him, the strength will come. He will prove himself to you and work in you that which is pleasing in His sight through Jesus Christ. It is important to be *willing* to walk in His ways. Do not think about waiting on God while in your heart you are not willing to be obedient. However weak you feel, only be willing, and He who has worked to *will*, will work to *do* by His power.

It may be that our consciousness of every weakness and

sin makes our text appear more of a hindrance than a help in waiting on God. But we have said more than once that the starting point and groundwork of this waiting is utter and absolute powerlessness. Put your faith in God's almighty power, and find in waiting on Him your deliverance. Any failure here will be because of efforts in your own strength. Come and learn that He is the God who is good and who alone can work any good thing. Be content to receive from God each moment of the day His grace to wait, to believe, and to see Him work all that is good in your life.

My soul, wait only on God!

Waiting on God for More Than We Know

And now, Lord, what do I wait for? My hope is in You. Deliver me from all my transgressions.

Psalm 39:7–8

There may be times when we do not know what we are waiting for, but we know we need to be in His presence. Other times we *think* we know, and it would be better to just wait on Him without an agenda. He is able to do for us immeasurably more than all we ask or think, and we are in danger of limiting Him when we always confine our desires and prayers to our own thoughts. It is a good thing at times to say with the psalmist, "And now, Lord, what do I wait for?" That is, I hardly know; I can only say, "My hope is in You."

We clearly see a limiting of God in the case of Israel. When Moses promised them meat in the wilderness, they doubted, saying, "Can God furnish a table in the wilderness? He struck the rock and the water gushed out. But can He also give us bread? Can He provide meat for His people?" If they had been asked whether God could provide streams in the desert, they would have answered yes. God had done it; He could do it again. But when the thought came that God might do something new, they limited Him. Their expectation could not rise beyond past experience or their own thoughts of what was possible. In the same way, we may limit God by our concept of what He has promised or what He is able to do. Let us be careful not to limit the Holy One of Israel by the way we pray. Let us believe that the very promises of God we claim have divine merit beyond our thought or imagination. Let us be confident of their fulfillment through His power, grace, and mercy. And then let us develop the habit of waiting on God not only for what we think we need but also for all He has promised to do for us.

In every true prayer there are two hearts involved. One is your heart with its small human expectation of what you need and what God can do. The other is God's great heart with its infinite, divine purposes for your blessing. Confess how little you understand what God wishes to do for you. Then wait on God to do more than you can ask or think.

You may have prayed to be delivered from temper, or pride, or self-will—and it seemed to be in vain. Could it be that you have limited God by your own thoughts about His power to do this or the way He will choose to deliver you? Worship the God who does wonders, who desires the best for you, and is able to give it. Bow before Him, waiting on Him until your soul envisions that you are in the hands of a powerful, wonder-working God. Let every longing and every prayer be one of asking God to do in you all that you ask and more.

In waiting on God, you may grow weary because you don't know what to expect. But be encouraged. Ignorance is often a good sign. He is teaching you to leave everything in His hands and to wait on Him alone.

My soul, wait only on God!

The Way to the New Song

*I waited patiently for the LORD; and He inclined to me,
and heard my cry. He has put a new song in my mouth;
praise to our God; many will see it and fear,
and will trust in the LORD.*

Psalm 40:1, 3

Listen to the testimony of one who can speak from experience of the sure and blessed outcome of patient waiting on God. True patience is so foreign to our self-confident nature, yet so indispensable to our waiting on God. It is an essential element of true faith, and we will once again meditate on what the Word has to teach us concerning it.

The word *patience* is derived from the Latin word for suffering. It suggests the thought of being under the constraint of some power from which we are eager to be free. At first we submit against our will. Then experience teaches us that when it is useless to resist, patient endurance is our wisest alternative. In waiting on God, it is important that we submit not because we are forced to, but because we want to be in the hands of our blessed Father. Patience becomes our highest blessing and our highest grace. It honors God and gives Him time to work His will in us. It is the highest expression of our faith in His goodness and faithfulness. It brings the soul perfect rest in the assurance that God is carrying on His work. It is the evidence of our consent that God deal with us in the way and time that He thinks best. True patience loses self-will to His perfect will.

Such patience is needed to truly wait on God. It is the growth and fruit of our first lessons in the school of waiting. To some it will seem strange how difficult it is to wait on God. The great stillness of soul before God that acknowledges its helplessness and waits for Him to reveal himself; the deep humility that does not allow one's own will or strength to work to any degree except as God works; the gentleness that is content to be and to know nothing except as God gives light; the entire resignation of the will that only wants to be a vessel through which His holy will can be revealed and accomplished—all these elements of patience are not found overnight. But they will come as the soul maintains its position and repeats, "Truly my soul silently waits for God; from Him comes my salvation. He only is my rock and my salvation; He is my defense; I shall not be greatly moved" (Psalm 62:1–2).

Have you ever noticed what proof we have that patience is a virtue for which very *special* grace is given? Paul says to the

Colossians: "strengthened with all might, according to His glorious power, for all patience and longsuffering with joy" (1:11). Yes, we need to be strengthened with God's might, strengthened as far as His glorious power reaches, if we are to wait on God in *all* patience. It is God revealing himself in us as our life and strength that will enable us with perfect patience to leave everything in His hands. If anyone is inclined to lose hope because he does not have such patience, be encouraged. It is in the process of our weak and imperfect waiting that God himself strengthens us and works out in us the patience of the saints, the patience of Christ himself.

Listen to the voice of one who was deeply tried: "I waited patiently for the LORD; and He inclined to me, and heard my cry" (Psalm 40:1). "He also brought me up out of a horrible pit, out of the miry clay, and set my feet upon a rock, and established my steps. He has put a new song in my mouth; praise to our God; many will see it and fear, and will trust in the LORD" (vv. 2–3). Patient waiting on God brings a rich reward; the deliverance is sure; God himself will put a new song in your mouth. Do not be impatient, whether it is in the exercise of prayer and worship that you find difficulty in waiting, or in persisting for an answer to prayer, or in the fulfilling of your heart's desire for the revelation of God himself in a deeper spiritual life. Don't be discouraged, but rest in the Lord, and wait patiently for Him. And if you sometimes feel patience is not your gift, remember it *is* God's gift. Take the prayer from 2 Thessalonians 3:5: "Now may the Lord direct your hearts into the love of God and into the patience of Christ." Into the patience with which you are to wait on God, He himself will guide you.

My soul, wait only on God!

Waiting on God for His Counsel

They soon forgot His works; they did not wait for His counsel.

Psalm 106:13

Our text refers to the sin of God's people in the wilderness. God had wonderfully redeemed them and was prepared to supply all their needs. But when needs arose "they did not wait for His counsel." They did not remember that the almighty God was their leader and provider; they did not ask what His plans were. They simply acted on their own thoughts and feelings and tempted and provoked God by their unbelief. "They did not wait for His counsel."

This is a common sin of God's people throughout history. In the land of Canaan in the days of Joshua, the three failures we read about were due to this sin: not waiting for God's guidance or counsel. In going against Ai, in making a covenant with the Gibeonites, in settling down without going up to possess the whole land—they did not wait for His counsel. Even the mature believer is in danger of this subtle temptation: looking at God's Word and interpreting it for himself without asking God for guidance. Let us take the warning and see what Israel teaches us. It is not only a danger to individuals but also to God's people collectively.

Our whole relationship to God is based on doing His will and being open to His leading. He has promised to make known His will to us by His Spirit, our guide into all truth. And our position is to be that of waiting for His counsel as the only guide for our thoughts and actions. In our church worship, in our prayer meetings, in our conventions, in our gatherings as managers, directors, committees, or helpers in any part of God's work, our first object should always be to find out what is on God's mind. God always works according to the counsel of His will. The more that counsel of His will is looked for and found and honored, the more surely and mightily will God do His work for us and through us.

The great danger in all these types of meetings is that having our Bible, our past experience of God's leading, our creed, and our honest desire to do God's will, we trust in these instead of fresh guidance. There may be elements of God's will, application of His Word, experience of His close presence and leading, and a manifestation of the power of His Spirit about which we know nothing. God is willing to open these up to those who are set on allowing Him to have His way and who are willing to wait for Him to make it known. When we come together, praising God for all He has done and taught and given, we may at the same time be limiting Him by not expecting greater things. It was when God had given the water out of the rock that they did not trust Him for bread. It was when God had given Jericho into his hands that Joshua thought the victory over Ai was sure and did not wait for counsel from God. And so while we think we know and trust the power of God for what we might expect, we may be hindering Him by not allowing time and by not practicing the habit of waiting for His counsel.

A minister has no duty more serious than teaching people to wait on God. Why was it that in the house of Cornelius, when Peter spoke these words, the Holy Spirit fell on all who heard the Word? (Acts 10:44). They had said, "Now therefore, we are all present before God, to hear all the things commanded you by God" (Acts 10:33). If there is no waiting for God's counsel, we may come together to give and to listen to the most fervent exposition of God's truth with little or no spiritual profit.

And so in all our gatherings we need to believe in the Holy Spirit as the guide and teacher of God's saints when they wait to be led by Him into the things that God has prepared, the things of which the heart on its own cannot conceive.

More stillness of soul to realize God's presence; more consciousness of ignorance of what God's great plans are; more faith in the certainty that God has greater things to show us, that He himself will be revealed in fresh glory—these must be the marks of the meetings of God's saints if they want to avoid the disgrace of not waiting for His counsel.

My soul, wait only on God!

His Light in the Heart

I wait for the LORD, my soul waits, and in His word I do hope. My soul waits for the LORD more than those who watch for the morning; yes, more than those who watch for the morning.

Psalm 130:5–6

There are times and situations in which dawn is awaited with intense longing: sailors in a shipwrecked vessel, a nighttime traveler in a dangerous country, an army that finds itself surrounded by an enemy are just a few examples. The morning light reveals what hope of escape there may be. In the same way, the saints of God living in the darkness of this world have longed for the light of His countenance—more than those who wait for the dawn. Can we say that we wait for God with this kind of fervency and expectancy? Our waiting on God can have no higher goal than to have His light shine on us and in us and through us all day.

God is light. Paul says, "For it is the God who commanded

light to shine out of darkness, who has shone in our hearts to give the light of the knowledge of the glory of God in the face of Jesus Christ" (2 Corinthians 4:6). Just as the sun shines its life-giving light on our Earth, so God shines in our hearts the light of His glory and His love. Our hearts are meant to have this light filling them every day.

How is this possible? Nature gives us the answer: Trees and flowers and grass do nothing to keep the sun shining on them; they simply exist and wait, and when the sunshine comes, they soak it up and benefit from it. The tiniest flower that lifts its head upward is met by the same radiance of light and blessing that illuminates the largest tree. We do not have to worry about the light we need for our day's work. The sun shines its light around us all day long. We simply expect it, receive it, enjoy it.

The only difference between nature's light and God's light is that what the trees and flowers do unconsciously, we are to do voluntarily and with loving acceptance. Simple faith in God's Word and His love opens the eyes and the heart to receive and enjoy the indescribable glory of His grace. And just as the trees, day-by-day and month-by-month, stand and grow into beauty and fruitfulness, absorbing whatever the sun gives, so it is the highest exercise of our Christian life to abide in the light of God and to allow it to fill us with the life and blessing it brings.

And if you still wonder if it is possible to enjoy as naturally as the trees enjoy the sun, the light of His love, I tell you that you most certainly can. From my breakfast table I look out on a beautiful valley with trees and vineyards and mountains in the distance. In our spring and autumn months the light in the morning is incomparable, and impulsively we say, "How beautiful!" The soul who will simply be still and wait on Him will see the incomparable beauty of His light and love every day.

Again, it is only learning to wait on Him—more than those who watch for the morning! Inside you may feel all is dark and empty. But that is the very best reason for waiting for the light of God. The first beginnings of light may be just enough to uncover the darkness and to humble you to confess any hidden sin. Can you trust the light to dispel the darkness? Believe that it will. Simply bow, even now, in stillness before God and wait on Him to shine in you. Say in humble faith, God is light, infinitely brighter and more beautiful than the light of the sun. God the Father is light. The Son is eternal, incomprehensible light. The Spirit is light concentrated and manifested—the light that enters and dwells and shines in our hearts. I have been so occupied with my own thoughts and efforts that I may not have opened the shutters to let His light in. Perhaps unbelief has kept it out. What would I think of a sun that could not shine? What of a God who does not shine? But He does. God is light! He must shine. It is His nature to shine. I will take time, simply be still, and rest in the light of God. I am weak, but I will wait on the Lord. The light will shine in me and make me full of light. And I shall learn to walk in the light and the joy of God. My soul waits on the Lord more than those who wait for the dawn.

My soul, wait only on God!

Waiting on God in Times of Darkness

And I will wait on the LORD, who hides His face from the house of Jacob; and I will hope in Him.

Isaiah 8:17

Here we have a servant of God waiting on Him not for himself but for his people, from whom God was hiding His face. It suggests to us how our waiting on God, though it begins with our personal needs or with the desire for a revelation of Him, does not need to stop there. We may be walking in the full light of God's approval, while God is hiding His face from His people around us. Far from being content to think that this is the punishment they deserve for their sin or the consequence of their indifference, we are called with tender hearts to think of their sad condition and to wait on God on their behalf. The privilege of waiting on God is one that brings with it great responsibility. Christ entered God's presence and at once used

His position of privilege and honor as intercessor. With the same determination, if we know what it is to enter in and wait on God, we must use our access for those who still live in darkness.

You no doubt worship with a certain congregation. Perhaps you are not finding the spiritual life or joy in the preaching or in the fellowship that you desire to find. Perhaps there is so much error or worldliness, or seeking after human wisdom and culture, or trust in formalities and observances, that you can easily see why God hides His face and why there is so little power for conversion or true edification. Then there are branches of Christian work with which you are connected—a Sunday school, an outreach committee, a men's prayer breakfast, a mission work abroad—in which the absence of the Spirit's working appears to indicate that God is hiding His face. You think you know the reason here, too. There is too much trust in men and money; too much formality and self-indulgence; too little faith and prayer; too little love and humility; too little of the spirit of the crucified Jesus. At times you feel as if things are hopeless; nothing will help.

Believe that God can and will help. Let the spirit of the prophet Isaiah come into you as you meditate on his words, and set yourself to wait on God on behalf of His people who have gone astray. Instead of feeling judgment, condemnation, or despair, realize your calling to wait on God. If others fail in doing it, give yourself to it all the more. The deeper the darkness, the greater the need to appeal to our one and only Deliverer. The more you see self-confidence in people around you, not knowing they are poor and miserable and blind, the more urgent the call is to you who profess to see the evil and have access to Him who alone can help, to be on your knees waiting on God. Each time you are tempted to criticize or shake your head in despair, say instead, "I will wait on the Lord."

There is yet a larger circle—the Christian church throughout the world. Think of Greek Orthodox, Roman Catholic, and Protestant churches and the condition of the millions that belong to them. Or think of only the Protestant churches with all their Bibles and orthodox creeds. There is so much ritual and tradition! So much rule of the flesh and of man in the very temple of God! This is a convincing proof that God does hide His face.

What are we to do who see this and are grieved? The first thing is to hear the psalmist: "I will wait on the Lord." We must wait on God, making humble confession of the sins of His people. We need to take *time* and wait on Him. Let us wait on God in tender, loving intercession for all believers, however wrong their lives or their teaching may appear. Wait on God in faith and expectation until He shows you that He hears. Let us wait on God with the simple offering of ourselves and with the sincere prayer that He will draw all men to himself. Let us wait on God and give Him no rest until He makes Zion a joy in the earth. Yes, rest in the Lord and wait patiently for Him who now hides His face from so many of His children. And let us say this: "I will wait on the LORD, who hides His face from the house of Jacob; and I will hope in Him."

My soul, wait only on God!

Waiting on God to Reveal Himself

And it will be said in that day: "Behold, this is our God;
we have waited for Him, and He will save us. This is
the LORD; we have waited for Him; we will be glad
and rejoice in His salvation."

Isaiah 25:9

In this passage we have two important thoughts: First, the language indicates God's people have been waiting on Him *together.* Second, the result of their waiting has been that God has revealed himself. They could joyfully respond, "Behold, this is our God. . . . This is the LORD." If we do not yet know the power and blessing of waiting together, we must learn it.

Note the phrase "We have waited for Him." It is repeated twice. In times of trouble the hearts of the people had been drawn together, and they had with one heart set themselves to wait for their God. Is not this what we need in our churches, conventions, and prayer meetings? The need of the church and the world demands it. There are conditions in the church of Christ to which no human wisdom is equal: ritualism, rationalism, formalism, and worldliness, to name a few—all robbing the church of its power. Culture, money, and pleasure threaten its spiritual life. Whatever power the church has is inadequate to cope with the power of unfaithfulness, disobedience, and dissatisfaction both in so-called Christian countries and in those where the gospel is not known. And yet is there not in the promises of God and in the power of the Holy Spirit provision made to meet these needs and give the church the assurance that she is doing all God expects of her? Would not waiting on God for the supply of His Spirit bring the needed blessing? There is no doubt it would.

The purpose of more structured waiting on God in our gatherings would be much the same as in personal worship. It would bring about a deeper conviction that God must and will do all; a more humble awareness of our helplessness and the need of our entire dependence on Him; a greater consciousness that the essential thing is to give God His place of honor and power. The purpose would also be to bring everyone in a praying and worshiping congregation to a deeper sense of God's presence, so that when they go their separate ways, they have a consciousness of having met God, of having left their requests with Him, and of knowing that together they can do what individually is not possible.

It is this experience that is indicated in our text. In a modern setting, God's people may become so conscious of His presence that in holy awe they will say, "This is our God . . . this is the LORD!" It is this experience, sadly enough, that is too often missing in our meetings of worship. The godly minister has no greater task than to lead his people into God's presence in preparation for the message from His Word. "We are all present before God" (Acts 10:33)—these words of Cornelius show that Peter's audience was prepared for the coming of the Holy Spirit. Waiting before God, waiting for God, and waiting on God make up the condition for God's showing His presence.

A congregation of believers gathers in prayer with this purpose: to wait or work through periods of silence together, to wait on God for corporate guidance, to discover together what God would have them do as a community of believers to reach the world around them, and to know the presence of God in their midst.

My soul, wait only on God!

The God of Judgment

*Yes, in the way of Your judgments, O LORD, we have waited
for You; the desire of our soul is for Your name and for the
remembrance of You. With my soul I have desired You in the
night, yes, by my spirit within me I will seek You early; for
when Your judgments are in the earth, the inhabitants
of the world will learn righteousness.*

Isaiah 26:8–9

*Therefore the LORD will wait, that He may be gracious to you;
and therefore He will be exalted, that He may have mercy
on you. For the LORD is a God of justice; blessed
are all those who wait for Him.*

Isaiah 30:18

God is a God of mercy and of judgment. All His dealings involve these two. We see mercy in the midst of judgment in the
time of the Flood, in the deliverance of Israel out of Egypt,
and in the overthrow of the Canaanites. We see it, too, in the
inner circle of His people. Judgment punishes sin, while mercy

saves the sinner. In waiting on God, we must beware of forgetting this. Though He is merciful, He is also a God of judgment. If we are honest in our longing for holiness, in our prayer to be wholly the Lord's, His holy presence will stir up and uncover hidden sin. It will bring us conviction of our sinful nature, its opposition to God's law, and its resistance to fulfill that law. The words will come true: "But who can endure the day of His coming? And who can stand when He appears? For He *is* like a refiner's fire" (Malachi 3:2). "Oh, that You would rend the heavens! That You would come down! That the mountains might shake at Your presence" (Isaiah 64:1–2). In great mercy God executes within the soul His judgments on sin, making the soul feel its guilt. Many try to flee these judgments. The soul that longs for God and for deliverance from sin bows under them in humility and in hope. In silence it says, "Rise up, O LORD! Let Your enemies be scattered" (Numbers 10:35). "In the way of Your judgments, O LORD, we have waited for You" (Isaiah 26:8).

No one who seeks to learn the blessed art of waiting on God should be surprised if at first the attempt to wait on Him only reveals more sin and darkness. Let no one despair because unconquered sin, evil thoughts, or discouragement appear to hide God's face. Even when His beloved Son, the gift and bearer of His mercy, was at Calvary, mercy was hidden for a time because of the sin He bore for us. Submit to the judgment of sin. Judgment prepares the way for mercy. It is written: "Zion shall be redeemed with justice, and her penitents with righteousness" (Isaiah 1:27). Wait on God in faith that

His tender mercy is working out His redemption. He will be gracious to you.

There is one more application of indescribable seriousness. We are expecting God *in judgment* to visit this earth: we are waiting for Him. We know of these coming judgments; we know that there are tens of thousands of "professing" Christians who live on in carelessness and who will perish if no change is made. Should we not warn them, plead for them, that perhaps God may have mercy on them? If we feel a lack of boldness, of zeal, of power, we should begin to wait on God for a revelation of His role as Judge, that we will speak and pray as never before. Waiting on God is not meant to be a spiritual self-indulgence. Its object is to let God and His holiness, Christ and His love, the Spirit and His fire take possession of us to warn and to stir up men with the message that we are waiting for a God not only of mercy but also of judgment.

My soul, wait only on God!

The God Who Waits on Us

> *Therefore the LORD will wait, that He may be gracious to you; and therefore He will be exalted, that He may have mercy on you. For the LORD is a God of justice; blessed are all those who wait for Him.*

Isaiah 30:18

We must think not only of *our* waiting on God but also of God's waiting on us. The vision of Him waiting on us will give new motivation and inspiration to our waiting on Him. It will give an indescribable confidence that our waiting is not in vain. If He waits for us, then we may be sure that we are more than welcome, that He rejoices to find those for whom He has been seeking. Let us seek even now, in the spirit of humble waiting on God, to find out something of what it means that the Lord waits to be gracious unto us, and in turn be blessed as we wait for Him.

Look up and see our great God on His throne. He is Love—a continuous and inexpressible desire to communicate His own goodness and blessedness to all His creatures. He longs and delights to bless. He has inconceivably glorious plans concerning each of His children to reveal in them His love and power by the power of His Holy Spirit. He waits with all the anticipation of a father's heart. He waits to be gracious to you. And each time you come to wait on Him, or seek to maintain in daily life the habit of waiting, you may look up and see Him ready to meet you.

You may ask, "How is it, if He waits to be gracious, that when I come and wait on Him, He does not always give the help I seek?" There is a twofold answer. The first is that God is a farmer. He waits for the precious fruit of the earth and has patience. He cannot gather the crop until it is ripe. He knows when we are spiritually ready to receive the blessing to our profit and His glory. Waiting in the sunshine of His love is what will ripen the soul for His blessing. Waiting under the cloud of trial that breaks in showers of blessing is essential. Be assured that if God waits longer to answer than you anticipated, it is only to make the blessing all the more precious. God waited four thousand years, until the fullness of time, before He sent His Son. Our times are in His hands. He will see that justice is done for His people. He wants to help us and will not delay one hour too long.

The second answer points to what has been said before. The Giver is more than the gift; God is more than the blessing; and our time spent waiting on Him is the only way to learn to find our life and joy in *Him*. If God's children only knew what a glorious God they have and what a privilege it is to be linked in fellowship with Him, they would leap for joy and tell the world. But the truth is we do not know this, or if we do, we don't believe it. Even when He keeps them waiting, they would learn to understand better than ever that His waiting is the highest proof of His graciousness.

Blessed are all they who wait for Him. A queen has her ladies-in-waiting. The position is one of subordination and service and yet it is also considered a position of the highest dignity and privilege, because a wise and gracious ruler makes them her companions and friends. What an honor and blessing to be attendants-in-waiting on the everlasting God, always on the watch for every indication of His will or favor, always conscious of His nearness, His goodness, and His grace. The Lord is good to those who wait for Him. Blessed are all those who wait for Him. It is a blessing when a waiting soul and a waiting God meet each other. God cannot do His work without waiting for the right time. Let waiting be our work as it is His. And if His waiting is nothing but goodness and graciousness, let ours be nothing but rejoicing in that goodness and confident expectancy of that grace. Let waiting represent to us pure blessing, because it brings us to a God who waits so that He may make himself known to us.

My soul, wait only on God!

The Almighty One

> *But those who wait on the LORD shall renew their strength;*
> *they shall mount up with wings like eagles, they shall run and*
> *not be weary, they shall walk and not faint.*

Isaiah 40:31

Waiting is affected by what we think of the one on whom we wait. Our waiting on God will depend greatly on our faith in who He is. Our text is the close of a passage in which God reveals himself as the everlasting and Almighty One. As that revelation enters our soul, the waiting will become the spontaneous expression of what we know Him to be—a God worthy to be waited on.

Listen to Isaiah: "Why do you say, O Jacob, and speak, O Israel: 'My way is hidden from the LORD, and my just claim is passed over by my God'?" (40:27). Why do you speak as if God does not hear or help?

"Have you not known? Have you not heard? The everlasting God, the LORD, the Creator of the ends of the earth, neither faints nor is weary. His understanding is unsearchable. He gives power to the weak, and to those who have no might He increases strength. Even the youths shall faint and be weary, and the young men shall utterly fall" (40:28–30). All that is considered by man to be strong will come to nothing. But those who wait on the Lord shall renew their strength.

The eagle is the king of birds and soars highest in the skies. Believers are to live a heavenly life in the presence and love and joy of God. They are to live where God lives and in His strength. To those who wait on Him, it shall be so.

Eagles are born with a potential power in their wings that surpasses all other birds. You are born of God. *You* have eagles' wings. God will teach you to use them.

Eagles are taught the use of their wings by their mothers. Imagine a cliff rising a thousand feet out of the sea. On a ledge high up on the rock the eagle builds her nest for her two young eaglets. When the time is right, the mother bird stirs up her nest, pushing the timid fledglings over the edge. They flutter and fall and sink toward the depths, but she swoops beneath them and bears them up on her own strong wings. And so they ride to a place of safety. Then she does it again, each time pushing them out over the edge and then swooping beneath them again until the eaglets become strong enough to fly on their own. "As an eagle stirs up its nest, hovers over its young, spreading out its wings, taking them up, carrying them on its wings, so the LORD alone led him" (Deuteronomy 32:11). The instinct of the mother eagle is God's gift, a picture of the love by which the Almighty trains His people to mount up as on eagles' wings.

He stirs up your nest. He prolongs your hopes. He tries your confidence. He makes you fear and tremble as all your strength fails and you feel utterly weary and helpless. And all the while He is spreading His strong wings beneath you to rest your weakness on and offering His everlasting strength to work in you. And all He asks is that you sink down in your weariness and *wait on Him* and allow Him in His Jehovah-strength to carry you as you ride on the wings of His omnipotence.

Dear believer, I beg you, lift up your eyes and *behold your God*! Listen to Him who says that He "neither faints nor is weary. His understanding is unsearchable" (Isaiah 40:28), who promises that you, too, will not faint or be weary, who asks nothing but this one thing: that you should *wait on Him*. And let your answer be, "On such a God, so mighty, so faithful, so tender—I will wait."

My soul, wait only on God!

The Certainty of Blessing

*Then you will know that I am the LORD, for they shall not be
ashamed who wait for Me.*

Isaiah 49:23

*Therefore the LORD will wait, that He may be gracious to you;
and therefore He will be exalted, that He may have mercy
on you. For the LORD is a God of justice; blessed are
all those who wait for Him.*

Isaiah 30:18

What promises! God seeks to get us to wait on Him by the
most positive assurances. He says it will *never* be in vain:
"They shall not be ashamed who wait for Me." It is strange
that though we should so often have experienced it we are still
slow to learn that this waiting must and can be the very breath
of our life, a continuous resting in God's presence and His
love, a constant yielding of ourselves to Him to perfect His
work in us. Let us once again listen and meditate until our

heart says with new conviction, "Blessed are all those who wait for Him!" In Day 6, we found in the prayer of Psalm 25: "Let no one who waits on You be ashamed." The fact that the prayer exists at all shows how we fear that we might be disappointed. Let us listen to God's answer until every fear is driven off and we send back to heaven the words God speaks.

The context of each of these two passages points us to times when God's church was in a very difficult situation, and to the human eye there were no possibilities of deliverance. But God intervenes with His word of promise and pledges His almighty power for the deliverance of His people. It is God himself who has undertaken the work of their redemption and invites them to wait on Him, assuring them that disappointment is impossible. We, too, are living in days in which there is much to mourn in the condition of the church: its hypocrisy and its staid traditionalism, to name two. Even with all we have to praise God for, there is, unfortunately, much to lament over in the church. If it were not for God's promises, we would have good reason to despair. But God has bound himself to us through His Word. He calls us to wait on Him. He assures us that we will not be put to shame. If our hearts could only learn to wait on Him until He reveals to us what His promises mean and what they show us about himself! May God increase the number of those who say, "Our soul waits for the LORD; He is our help and our shield" (Psalm 33:20).

This waiting on God on behalf of His church and His people will depend greatly on the place that waiting on Him has in our personal life. Our minds may often have beautiful visions of what God has promised to do and our lips may speak of them in eloquent words, but these are not the measure of our faith or power. It is, rather, what we know of God in our personal experience: conquering the enemies within, reigning, ruling, and revealing himself in His holiness and power in our inmost being. It is this revelation that will be the true measure of the spiritual blessing we expect from Him and bring to others. It is as we know how waiting on God can bless our own souls that we will confidently hope for the blessing to come to the church around us. The promised blessings for us and for others may be delayed, but knowing Him who has promised makes the wait worthwhile and full of hope. Be sure to allow this truth to take full possession of your soul: Waiting on God is the highest privilege of His redeemed child.

In the same way that the sunshine enters with its light and warmth, its beauty and blessing, every little blade of grass that rises out of the cold earth, so the everlasting God meets, in the greatness and the tenderness of His love, each waiting child to shine in their heart "the light of the knowledge of the glory of God in the face of Jesus Christ" (2 Corinthians 4:6). Read these words again until your heart learns to know what God waits to do for you. Who can measure the difference between the great sun and that little blade of grass? And yet the grass has all of the sun it needs or can hold. While waiting on God, believe that His greatness and your smallness suit each other wonderfully. Just bow in your emptiness and poverty, your powerlessness and humility, and surrender to His will. As you wait on Him, God will come near. He will reveal himself as the God who faithfully fulfills every one of His promises. Let your heart continue to repeat this promise: "Blessed are all those who wait for Him."

My soul, wait only on God!

Waiting on God for Inconceivable Things

For since the beginning of the world men have not heard nor perceived by the ear, nor has the eye seen any God besides You, who acts for the one who waits for Him.

Isaiah 64:4

The American Standard Version of our text emphasizes how God *works* for those who wait on Him. The King James Version speaks of *what* God has prepared for us. Our responsibility is to wait on God. What will then be revealed is beyond what the human heart can conceive. Whether it is *what* He has prepared or what He will *do* for us, either is more than we who are finite human beings should expect from an almighty God. But He wants us to expect it. He wants us to believe and trust Him for the impossible.

The previous verses, especially from Isaiah 63:15–64:2, refer to the low state of God's people. The prayer has been poured out, "Look down from heaven" (v. 15). "Why have you . . . hardened our heart from Your fear? Return for Your servants' sake" (v. 17). And 64:1–2 is still more urgent, "Oh, that You would rend the heavens! That You would come down! That the mountains might shake at Your presence; as fire burns brushwood, as fire causes water to boil; to make Your name known to Your adversaries, that the nations may tremble at Your presence!" Then follows the plea from the past: "When You did awesome things for which we did not look, You came down, the mountains shook at Your presence" (v. 3). Now we will see the faith that has been awakened by the thought of things that had not been looked for. He is still the same God: "For . . . men have not heard nor perceived by the ear, nor has the eye seen any God besides You, who acts for the one who waits for Him" (v. 4). God alone knows what He can do for His waiting people. As Paul explains and applies it: "For what man knows the things of a man except the spirit of the man which is in him? Even so no one knows the things of God except the Spirit of God" (1 Corinthians 2:11). But God has revealed them to us by His Spirit.

The need of God's people, and the call for God's intervention, is as urgent in our day as it was in the time of Isaiah. There is now as there was then, as there always has been, a remnant who seek after God with their whole heart. But if we look at Christians as a whole, at the condition of the church of Christ, there is infinite reason to ask God to rend the heavens and come down. Nothing but a special intervention of almighty power will accomplish what is needed. I don't think we have a right concept of what the so-called Christian world is in the sight of God. Unless God comes down "to make His name known to His adversaries," our labors are comparatively fruitless. Look at ministry. So much of it is done by the wisdom of man. So little is in demonstration of the Spirit and of power. Think of the unity of the body—how little there is of the manifestation of the power of a heavenly love binding God's children into one. Think of holiness—by that I mean the holiness of Christlike humility and death to the world— how little the world sees that there are men and women among them who live in Christ and in whom Christ lives.

What can be done? There is only one thing. We must wait on God. We must cry with a cry that never rests: "Oh that You would rend the heavens and come down, that the mountains might flow down at Your presence!" We must desire and believe, we must ask and expect, that God will do what is inconceivable. The miracle-working God, who surpasses all our expectations, must be the God of our confidence.

Yes, let God's people enlarge their hearts to wait on a God able to do much more than they can ask or think. Let us band ourselves together as His chosen people who cry day and night to Him for things humankind has not yet seen. He is able to make a name for His people on the earth. He will be gracious unto you. Blessed are all those who wait for Him.

My soul, wait only on God!

Seeking to Know His Goodness

The LORD is good to those who wait for Him,
to the soul who seeks Him.

Lamentations 3:25

"No one is good but One, *that is,* God" (Matthew 19:17). "Your mercy, O LORD, is in the heavens; Your faithfulness reaches to the clouds" (Psalm 36:5). "Oh, how great is Your goodness, which You have laid up for those who fear You, which You have prepared for those who trust in You" (Psalm 31:19). "Oh, taste and see that the LORD is good; blessed is the man who trusts in Him!" (Psalm 34:8). The *way* of entering into and rejoicing in this goodness of God is made clear in our text: waiting for Him and seeking Him. The Lord is good. But His own children often do not truly *know* the blessing of His goodness, because they do not wait in quietness for Him to reveal it. Those souls who do wait, know it to be true. You might think those who wait would be those who doubt. But this is only when they do *not* wait—and are impatient for God to act. Do you want to know the goodness of God? Give yourself to a life of waiting on Him.

When we first enter the school of waiting on God, our hearts are chiefly set on His blessings. God graciously uses our need and desire for help to educate us for something higher than we may have been thinking of. We were seeking gifts; He longs to give himself and to satisfy the soul with His goodness. It is for this reason that He often withholds the gifts and that the time of waiting seems long. He is always seeking to win the hearts of His children for himself. He hopes that we will not only say when He gives the gift, "How good God is!" but that long before it comes, and even if it never comes, we will always experience the fact that it is good to wait on God. *He* is worth waiting for.

What a blessed life the life of waiting becomes: it is a continual worship of faith, adoring and trusting His goodness. As your soul learns this secret, every act or exercise of waiting becomes a quiet entering into the goodness of God to let it do its blessed work and satisfy all your needs. And every experience of God's goodness gives the work of waiting new attractiveness. Instead of taking refuge only when we are in need, there will come a great longing to simply wait in His presence. And however our daily duties and responsibilities occupy our time and our minds, our souls will become more familiar with the secret art of waiting. It will become the habit and attitude of the soul.

Are you beginning to grasp the fact that waiting is not one of a number of Christian characteristics to be thought of from time to time, but rather an attitude that lies at the root of the Christian life? Waiting gives a higher value and a new power to our prayer and worship, to our faith and surrender, because it links us to God in inseparable dependence.

Let me urge you to take the time and trouble to develop this much-needed element of the Christian life. We get too much of our Christian teaching secondhand. That teaching has value—like John the Baptist's, which directed his disciples away from himself to the living Christ—only if it leads us to God himself. What we need is *more of God*. We tend to be more occupied with our work than anything else. As with Martha, the very service we want to give to the Master separates us from Him. It is neither pleasing to Him nor profitable to us. The more we work, the more we need to wait on God. When we believe this truth, the doing of God's will, instead of exhausting us, will be our nourishment and refreshment and strength. "The LORD is good to those who wait for Him." *How* good can only be told by those who wait.

My soul, wait only on God!

Waiting Quietly

*It is good that one should hope and wait quietly for
the salvation of the LORD.*

Lamentations 3:26

"Take heed, and be quiet; do not fear or be fainthearted" (Isaiah 7:4). "In returning and rest you shall be saved; in quietness and confidence shall be your strength" (Isaiah 30:15). Verses like these bring to our attention the close connection between quietness and faith and show us what a deep need there is for quietness as an element of true waiting on God. If we are to have our whole heart turned toward God, we must turn it away from created things, from all that would unduly occupy our time and hold our interest.

God is so full of infinite greatness and glory, and we are so far removed from Him, that it takes our whole heart and desire to in some small way know and receive Him. Everything that is not of God, that excites our fears, or stirs our efforts, or awakens our hopes, or makes us glad, stands in the way of our perfect waiting on Him.

The very thought of God in His majesty and holiness should silence us. Over and over the Scriptures tell this truth: "But the LORD is in His holy temple. Let all the earth keep silence before Him" (Habakkuk 2:20). "Be silent in the presence of the Lord GOD" (Zephaniah 1:7). "Be silent, all flesh, before the LORD, for He is aroused from His holy habitation!" (Zechariah 2:13).

As long as waiting on God is thought of only as a step toward more productive prayer and the obtaining of requests, we will not know the blessing of time with God for the sake of fellowship with Him. But when we realize that waiting on God is a blessing in itself, our adoration of Him will humble us, making the way open for God to speak to us and reveal himself. "The lofty looks of man shall be humbled, the haughtiness of men shall be bowed down, and the LORD alone shall be exalted in that day" (Isaiah 2:11).

Everyone who wants to learn the art of waiting on God must "take heed, and be quiet"(Isaiah 7:4); "It is good that one should hope and wait quietly" (Lamentations 3:26). Take time to be away from friends, from duties, from cares and joys; time to be still and quiet before God. Give the Word and prayer high priority; but remember, even these good things may get in the way of simply waiting. The activity of the mind needed to study the Word and to put thoughts into prayer, and the activity of the heart with its desires and hopes and fears, may distract us from waiting on the One who knows our mind and heart. Our whole being is not allowed to become prostrate in silence before Him. Though at first it may be difficult to set aside these activities for a time, every effort to do so will be rewarded. We will find that this kind of waiting gives peace and renewed energy we have not known.

One reason that it is good to learn to wait quietly before the Lord without speaking is that it acknowledges our inability to receive blessing from God on our own. The blessing will not come by our "willing" or "running," or even by our thinking and praying, but by our waiting in His presence. By waiting we confess our trust that God will in His time and in His way come to our aid.

My soul, wait only on God!

Waiting in Holy Expectancy

Therefore I will look to the LORD; I will wait for the God of my salvation; my God will hear me.

Micah 7:7

A little book I read some time ago contained one of the best sermons I have seen on the text of this chapter. It told of a king who prepared a city for some of his poor subjects. Not far from their homes were large storehouses, where everything they could possibly need was supplied if they would only send in their requests. There was just one condition: that they be on the lookout to receive the answer to their request, so that when the king's messengers came with supplies, they would always be found waiting and ready to receive them. The sad story goes on to tell of one despondent subject who never expected to get what he asked for because he felt too unworthy. One day he was taken to the king's storehouses, and there to his amazement he saw all the packages addressed to him. Deliveries had been attempted, but the packages always came back. There was the garment of praise, and the oil of joy, and the eye salve he had asked for, and so much more. The messengers had been to his door, but always found it closed and no one around to receive the packages. From that time on the poor man learned the lesson Micah still teaches us today: "I will look to the LORD; I will wait for the God of my salvation; my God will hear me."

We have said more than once that waiting for a specific answer to prayer is not the whole process of waiting, but only a part. Today we want to emphasize that it *is* a part, and a very important one. When we have made special requests to God, our waiting must involve the confidence that God hears us. Holy, joyful expectancy is the very essence of true waiting. This type of expectancy applies not only to the varied requests every believer makes but especially to the one request that ought to be the primary thing we all seek: that the life of God in the soul may have full control. Expecting that Christ may be fully formed within and that we may be filled with all the fullness of God. This is what God has promised yet it is what God's people rarely seek, most often because they do not believe it is possible. But we ought to seek it and dare to expect it, because God is able and waiting to work it in us.

It is important to remember that it is *God* who works in us. For this to happen, our efforts must cease. Our hope must be in the work of God, who raised Jesus from the dead. Our waiting must become more than ever a lingering before God in stillness of soul, depending on Him who raises the dead and calls the things that are not as though they were.

Notice how the threefold use of the name of God in our text points us to the One who alone delivers our expectation. "I will look to the LORD; I will wait for the God of my salvation; my God will hear me." Everything that has to do with salvation, everything that is good and holy, must be the direct, personal work of God within us. Every moment of a life in the will of God must be of His working. I have only to look to Him, to wait for Him, and to know that He hears me.

God says, "Be still, and know that I am God" (Psalm 46:10).

There is no stillness like that of the grave. Jesus, by His death, taught us death to self with its own will and wisdom, its own strength and energy: this is real rest. As we deny self, our soul becomes still before God and He will reveal himself to us. "Then He arose and rebuked the wind, and said to the sea, 'Peace, be still!' And the wind ceased and there was a great calm" (Mark 4:39). And the disciples knew who He was as never before.

My soul, wait only on God!

Waiting on God for Redemption

There was a man in Jerusalem whose name was Simeon, and this man was just and devout, waiting for the Consolation of Israel, and the Holy Spirit was upon him. . . . Now there was one, Anna, a prophetess . . . [who] spoke of Him to all those who looked for redemption in Jerusalem.

Luke 2:25, 36, 38

Here we have the marks of a waiting believer. *Just*, righteous in all his conduct; *devout*, devoted to God and always walking in His presence; *waiting for the Consolation of Israel*, looking for the fulfillment of God's promises: *and the Holy Spirit was upon him*. Through devoted waiting, Simeon was prepared for the blessing. Anna spoke of Him to all who looked for redemption in Jerusalem. The mark of a godly group of men and women in Jerusalem, in the middle of surrounding formalism and worldliness, was that they were waiting on God and looking for His promised redemption.

Now that the Consolation of Israel has come and our redemption has been accomplished, will our waiting differ from those who looked forward to it? Yes, in two aspects. We wait on God in the full power of the redemption, but we still wait for its full revelation.

Christ said, "At that day you will know that I am in My Father, and you in Me, and I in you. Abide in Me, and I in you. As the branch cannot bear fruit of itself, unless it abides in the vine, neither can you, unless you abide in Me" (John 14:20; 15:4). The New Testament teaches us to present ourselves to God "to be dead indeed to sin, but alive to God in Christ Jesus our Lord" (Romans 6:11). "Blessed be the God and Father of our Lord Jesus Christ, who has blessed us with every spiritual blessing in the heavenly places in Christ" (Ephesians 1:3). Our waiting on God is now in the wonderful knowledge, confirmed in us by the Holy Spirit, that we are accepted in the beloved, that the love that rests on Him rests on us, and that we are living in that love in the actual presence of God. The old saints took their stand on the Word of God. Waiting and hoping on that Word, we, too, rest on it—but it is a far greater privilege to be joined to Christ Jesus! In our waiting on God, let this be our confidence: In Christ we have access to the Father; our waiting is never in vain.

Christ not only said, "Abide in Me," but also *and I in you.* The New Testament not only speaks of our being *in Christ* but also of Christ being *in us*, the greatest mystery of redeeming love. As we maintain our place in Christ day by day, God reveals Christ through us. His mind and attitude and likeness take on form and substance in us, so that each believer can truly say, "Christ lives in me" (Galatians 2:20).

My life in Christ and Christ's life in me complement each other. The more my waiting on God is marked by my living faith that I am in Christ, the more I will thirst for Christ in me. And the waiting on God that began with special needs and requests will increasingly become a revelation of His redemption in me.

Our waiting differs from the old saints in the sense of our position on this side of redemption, but it is the same in the sense that we wait on the same God, who alone delivers our expectations.

Learn from Simeon and Anna. It was impossible for them to do anything toward the great redemption—the birth of Christ, His death, and resurrection. It was God's work. They could do nothing but wait. And we are as helpless concerning the revelation of Christ in us. God did not work out our redemption in Christ as a whole and then leave the details of its application to us.

The revelation of Christ in every individual believer, step-by-step and moment-by-moment, is as much the work of God's almighty power as was Jesus' sacrifice for us. Until this truth dawns on us, we will not know the full blessing of waiting on Him. We are just as dependent on God for the revelation of redemption in us as were the saints of old in their anticipation of it. The sense of complete and absolute powerlessness, and the confidence that God can and will do all, must be the marks of our waiting on God today. As gloriously as God proved himself in the past as the faithful and wonder-working God, He will prove himself to us.

My soul, wait only on God!

Waiting for the Coming of His Son

*Be like men who wait for their master, when he will return
from the wedding, that when he comes and knocks
they may open to him immediately.*

Luke 12:36

*Keep this commandment without spot, blameless until our Lord
Jesus Christ's appearing, which He will manifest in His own
time, He who is the blessed and only Potentate,
the King of kings and Lord of lords.*

1 Timothy 6:14–15

*For they themselves declare concerning us what manner of entry
we had to you, and how you turned to God from idols to serve
the living and true God, and to wait for His Son from heaven,
whom He raised from the dead, even Jesus who delivers
us from the wrath to come.*

1 Thessalonians 1:9–10

Waiting on God and waiting for His Son were both initiated

in view of the other and cannot be separated. Waiting on God for His presence and power in our daily life is the only true preparation for waiting for Christ in humility and true holiness. Waiting for Christ's coming to take us to heaven gives waiting on God its tone of hopefulness and joy. The Father, who in His own time will reveal His Son from heaven, is the God who, as we wait on Him, prepares us for the revelation of His Son. This present life and the coming glory are inseparably connected in God and in us.

Sometimes there is the danger of separating them. It is always easier to dwell on an experience in the past or look forward to something in the future than to live faithfully in the present. As we think about what God has done in the past or will do in the future, the claim on our lives for present obligations and submission to His will may be neglected. Waiting on God must always lead to waiting for Christ to do a present work. There is also the temptation to look forward to future events rather than the single fact of His coming. In the study of coming events, imagination and reason tend to overshadow a humble waiting on God, loving Him, and anticipating His appearing. All who claim to wait for Christ's coming must wait on God now. The anticipation of that glorious appearing will strengthen you to wait on God for what He is to do presently in you.

"Looking for the blessed hope and glorious appearing of our great God and Savior Jesus Christ" (Titus 2:12–13) is one of the great bonds uniting God's church throughout the ages. "He comes, in that Day, to be glorified in His saints and to be admired among all those who believe" (2 Thessalonians 1:10). Then we will all meet, and the unity of the body of Christ will be seen in its divine glory. It will be the meeting place and the satisfaction of God's love: Jesus receiving His people and presenting them to the Father; His people meeting Him and worshiping Him as never before; His people meeting each other in the bond of God's love. Let us wait, long for, and love the appearing of our Lord and heavenly Bridegroom.

Tender love to Him and to each other is the true and only bridal spirit. This is sometimes overlooked. Some speak about the expectancy of faith as being the true sign of the bride. Risking criticism, I express my disagreement. An unworthy bride, about to be married to a prince, might be thinking only of the position and the riches she is to receive. In the same way, the expectancy of faith might be very strong, while true love is completely absent. We are not in the bride's place when we are deep into the study of prophetic subjects, but when in humility and love we are clinging to our Lord and to His people. Jesus refuses to accept our love unless it is expressed also to His disciples. Waiting for His coming means waiting for the glorious unity of the body while we attempt to maintain that unity in humility and love here on earth. Those who love most are the most ready for His coming. Love to each other is the life and beauty of His bride, the church.

And how is this to be brought about? Beloved child of God, if you want to learn the right way to wait for His Son from heaven, live your life waiting on God. Remember how Jesus lived waiting on God. He could do nothing by himself.

It was God who perfected His Son through suffering and then exalted Him. It is God alone who can give you the deep spiritual life of one who is truly waiting for His Son: wait on God for it. Waiting for Christ is very different from waiting for things that may come to pass. The latter, any Christian can do; the former, God must work in you every day by His Holy Spirit. Therefore, all of you who wait on God, look to Him for grace to wait for His Son from heaven in the Spirit that is from heaven. And you who want to wait for His Son, wait on God continually to reveal Christ in you.

The revelation of Christ in us, which is given to those who wait on God, is the true preparation for the full revelation of Christ in glory.

My soul, wait only on God!

Waiting for the Promise of the Father

*He commanded them not to depart from Jerusalem, but to
wait for the Promise of the Father, "which," He said,
"you have heard from Me."*

Acts 1:4

When through Simeon and Anna we looked at the saints in
Jerusalem at the time of Christ's birth, we saw how, though
the redemption they waited for has since come, the call to
waiting is no less urgent for us than it was for them. We wait
for the full revelation in us of what they could hardly compre-
hend. It is the same with waiting for the promise of the Father.
In one sense, the fulfillment can never come again as it came
at Pentecost. In another sense, we need to wait for the Father
to fulfill His promise in us with as deep a reality as it was with
the first disciples.

The Holy Spirit is not a person distinct from the Father in

the way two persons on earth are distinct. The Father and the Spirit are never without or separate from each other. The Father is always in the Spirit; the Spirit works nothing except what the Father works in Him. Each moment the same Spirit that is in us is in God, too. He who is full of the Spirit will be the most apt to wait on God more earnestly. The Spirit in us is not a power at our disposal. Nor is the Spirit an independent power, acting apart from the Father and the Son. The Spirit is the actual living presence and power of the Father working in us. The one who knows the Spirit is in him will wait on the Father for the full revelation and experience of the Spirit's indwelling.

We can see this in what the apostles experienced. They were filled with the Spirit at Pentecost (Acts 2). Not long after this, having returned from the council where they had been forbidden to preach, they prayed once more for boldness to speak in His name, and a fresh outpouring of the Holy Spirit showed the Father's increased fulfillment of His promise (Acts 4).

At Samaria, by the Word and the Spirit, many had been converted and the whole city filled with joy (Acts 8). Hearing the apostles' prayer, the Father once again fulfilled the promise, this time to the waiting group in Cornelius's house (Acts 10). We see the Spirit increasing a fifth time in Acts 13. It was when men filled with the Spirit prayed and fasted that the promise of the Father was freshly fulfilled and the leading of the Spirit was given from heaven: "Separate to Me Barnabas and Saul for the work to which I have called them" (Acts 13:2).

Also, in Ephesians, we find Paul praying for those who have been sealed with the Spirit, that God would give them the spirit of illumination and "that He would grant [them], according to the riches of His glory, to be strengthened with might through His Spirit in the inner man" (3:14–16).

The Spirit given at Pentecost was not a project that God failed with in heaven and so sent to earth. God does not give away anything in that sense. When He gives grace, or strength, or life, He gives it by giving himself. His gifts are inseparable from himself. It is all the more true with the Holy Spirit. He is God—present and working in us. The only way to see more of His work is to wait on the Father.

This gives new meaning and promise to our life of waiting. It teaches us to maintain the place where the disciples waited at the footstool of the throne. It reminds us of how helpless they were to meet their enemies or to preach to Christ's enemies until they were given power. So we also can only be strong in the life of faith or the work of love when we are in direct communication with God and Christ and they maintain the life of the Spirit in us. The Spirit's manifestation in us assures us that God, through Christ, will work in us to bring to pass that which is unexpected, and even impossible. There is nothing the church cannot do if her members will learn to wait on God. The promise of the Father, once so gloriously fulfilled but still unexhausted, accomplishes impossibilities when the church denies self and the world in favor of love.

Let each of us meditate on this inconceivably great truth: The Father waits to fill the church with the Holy Spirit—and He is ready to fill *me*!

With this faith let there come over the soul a quiet and holy fear as it waits in quietness to take it all in. And let your life increasingly become full of deep joy in the hope of the ever-increasing fulfillment of the Father's promise.

My soul, wait only on God!

Waiting Continually

*So you, by the help of your God, return; observe mercy and
justice, and wait on your God continually.*

Hosea 12:6

Continuity is an essential element of biological life. Interrupt
it in a man, and all is lost; he is dead. Continuity is also essential to a healthy Christian life. God wants me to live: physically
and spiritually. I want to live physically. How badly do I want
to live spiritually? If waiting on God is the essence of true
Christianity, the maintenance of an attitude of entire dependence on Him must be continual. The command of God,
"Wait on your God continually," must be embraced and
obeyed. There may be times of special waiting. But the attitude and habit of the soul must be unchangeable and uninter-
rupted.

Waiting continually on God is a necessity to maintain spiritual life. To those who are content with a *nominal* Christian
life, it will appear as a special call, something beyond the es-

sentials. But all who pray, "Lord, make me holy as you are holy; keep me as near to you as it is possible for me to be; fill me as full of your love as I can contain," know that it is an absolute priority. They know that there can be no unbroken fellowship with God, no full abiding in Christ, no maintaining of victory over sin and readiness for service without waiting continually on the Lord.

Waiting continually *is* a possibility. Many think that our crowded lives make it impossible. They feel they cannot always be thinking of it. This is because they do not understand that it is a matter of the heart, and that what the heart is full of, occupies it, even when our thoughts are on other things. A father's heart may be filled continually with intense love and longing for a sick wife or child at home, even though pressing business requires all his thoughts. When the heart has learned how entirely powerless it is to keep itself or to produce any good; when it has learned how surely and absolutely God will keep it; when it has, in despair of itself, accepted God's promise to do for it the impossible; it learns to rest in God and, in the midst of occupations and temptations, waits continually.

God's commands are enablers; His "rules of conduct" are promises, a revelation of what He will do for us. When you first begin waiting on God, it is with frequent intermission and some failure. But remember that God is watching over you in love and is strengthening you in it. There are times when waiting appears to be simply a waste of time; be assured it is not. He who calls you to wait on Him sees your weak efforts and uses them. Your spiritual life is not your own work;

it is God's. He asks only a willing, waiting heart. It is God's Spirit who has begun the work and who will complete it.

If we wait, He will work.

And now we are coming to the end of our meditations. It is vitally important that you and I learn one lesson: God will work in us continually. But the experience can be blocked by unbelief. He who by His Spirit teaches you to wait continually will also allow you to experience His blessing. In the love and the life and the work of God there can be no break or interruption.

Do not limit God by your thoughts of what may be expected. Fix your eyes on this one truth: God in His very nature as the giver of life cannot do otherwise than every moment work in His child. Do not say, "If I wait continually, God will work continually." Rather, turn it around and say, "God works continually; I may wait on Him continually." Take time to catch the vision of God working continually—without a moment's intermission. Then your waiting continually will come naturally. Full of trust and joy, the habit of the soul will be: "On You I wait all the day" (Psalm 25:5).

My soul, wait only on God!

Waiting Only on God

*My soul, wait silently for God alone, for my expectation is
from Him. He only is my rock and my salvation;
He is my defense; I shall not be moved.*

Psalm 62:5–6

It is possible to wait continually on God while not waiting *only*
on Him. There may be secret confidences that hinder us and
also prevent the expected blessing. And so the word *only* is
important to the fullness and certainty of blessing. "My soul,
wait silently for God *alone.* . . . He *only* is my rock" (emphasis
added).

There is only one God, one source of life and happiness
for the heart. You desire to be good. "No one *is* good but One,
that is, God" (Matthew 19:17), and there is no possible goodness except what is received directly from Him. You have tried
to be holy. "No one is holy like the LORD, for there is none
besides You, nor is there any rock like our God" (1 Samuel
2:2), and there is no holiness except what He breathes in you

by His Spirit. You would live and work for God and His kingdom, for men and their salvation. "Have you not known? Have you not heard? The everlasting God, the LORD, the Creator of the ends of the earth, neither faints nor is weary. His understanding is unsearchable. He gives power to the weak, and to those who have no might He increases strength. Those who wait on the LORD shall renew their strength" (Isaiah 40:28–29, 31).

You will not find many who can help you in this. There will be plenty of fellow Christians who will entice you to put your trust in churches and doctrines, in schemes and plans and human devices, in special men of God, and in special ways of receiving grace. "He removed the high places and broke the sacred pillars, cut down the wooden image and broke in pieces the bronze serpent that Moses had made; for until those days the children of Israel burned incense to it, and called it Nehushtan" (2 Kings 18:4). The ark and the temple gave false confidence. Let the living God alone, and none other but He, be your hope.

Eyes and hands and feet, mind and thought, may be intently engaged in the duties of this life, but your innermost being—your heart—can still be involved in waiting on God continually. You are an immortal spirit, created not for this world but for eternity and for God. Know your privilege. Wait on God. Let nothing take its place.

Our two greatest enemies are the world and self. Let no earthly satisfaction or enjoyment, however innocent, keep you from going to God for the deepest joy and contentment.

Pleasing self in little things may strengthen it to assert itself in greater things. Let your expectation be from God alone. Whatever your spiritual or physical need, whatever the desire or prayer of your heart, whatever your interest in connection with God's work in the church or in the world—let your expectations be from Him.

Never forget the two foundational truths on which this blessed waiting rests. If you are ever inclined to think that "waiting only" is too hard or too high, these truths will recall you at once. They are: your absolute helplessness and God's absolute sufficiency.

Examine deeply the sinfulness of all that is of self. Look closely at your complete and constant impotence to ever change yourself or to generate anything that is spiritually good. Evaluate carefully your relationship of dependence upon God. Let your heart move deeper still into His covenant of redemption with His promise to restore more gloriously than ever what you have lost and by His Son and His Spirit to give you unceasingly all that you need of His presence and power.

No words can tell or heart conceive the riches of the glory of this mystery of the Father and of Christ. Our God, in the infinite tenderness and almighty power of His love, waits to be our life and our joy.

"My soul, wait silently for God alone, for my expectation is from Him" (Psalm 62:5).

My soul, wait only on God!

Author's Note

William Law wrote a book on the Holy Spirit called *The Power of the Spirit.** In the Preface I have said how much I owe to the book. What this author puts more clearly than I have found anywhere else are these cardinal truths:

1. The very nature and being of God, as the only possessor and dispenser of any life there is in the universe, implies that He must continually communicate to every creature the power by which it exists. Therefore, He must all the more communicate the power by which a being can do that which is good.

2. The very nature and being of a creature, as owing its existence to God alone, and equally owing to Him each moment the continuation of that existence, implies that its hap-

---

*A humble, earnest, and affectionate address to the clergy. Out of print.

piness can be found only in absolute, unceasing, and momentary dependence on God.

3. The great value and blessing of the gift of the Spirit at Pentecost, as the fruit of Christ's redemption, is that it is now possible for God to take possession of His redeemed children and work in them as He did in Adam before the Fall. We need to know the Holy Spirit as the presence and power of God in us restored to their true place.

4. In the spiritual life, our great need is to acknowledge two great lessons. The one is our entire sinfulness and helplessness—our complete inability by any effort of our own to do anything toward the maintenance and increase of our inner spiritual life. The other is the infinite willingness of God's love, which is nothing but a desire to communicate himself and His blessedness to us, to meet our every need and every moment to work in us by His Son and Spirit what we need.

5. Therefore, the very essence of true religion, whether in heaven or on earth, consists in an unalterable dependence on God, because we can give God no other glory than to yield ourselves to His love, which created us to display in us its glory that it may now perfect its work in us.

I do not need to point out how deeply these truths go to the very root of the spiritual life, especially the life of waiting on God.

ARE YOU READY TO BE CHANGED?

Life Lessons to Be Learned From the Bible's Gardens

Jane Rubietta is holding open a gate to the two most important gardens in the Bible—Eden and Gethsemane—and allowing you take the ultimate soul-journey. Masterfully weaving together the analogy of our souls as gardens with God as our caretaker, she provides Scripture passages and special insight into both Eden and Gethsemane to challenge you to experience personal growth and new life.

Between Two Gardens, by Jane Rubietta

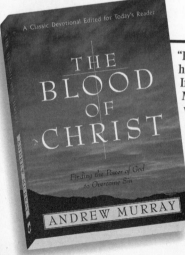

A Lesson on the Foundation of Faith

"Power in the blood," is a phrase most Christians have heard many times but don't truly understand. In *The Blood of Christ*, master theologian Andrew Murray takes a step-by-step approach to teaching why the blood of Christ has unparalleled power and exploring the promises given to believers through the shedding of the blood. This is a book no Christian should overlook for grasping the truth of redemption.

The Blood of Christ, by Andrew Murray

◊ BETHANYHOUSE
11400 Hampshire Avenue S.
Bloomington, MN 55438
www.bethanyhouse.com
(800) 328-6109

Thank you for selecting a book from
BETHANY HOUSE PUBLISHERS

Bethany House Publishers is a ministry of Bethany Fellowship International, an interdenominational, nonprofit organization committed to spreading the Good News of Jesus Christ around the world through evangelism, church planting, literature distribution, and care for those in need. Missionary training is offered through Bethany College of Missions.

Bethany Fellowship International is a member of the National Association of Evangelicals and subscribes to its statement of faith. If you would like further information, please contact:

Bethany Fellowship International
6820 Auto Club Road
Minneapolis, MN 55438 USA